JANE GOODALL

Animal Scientist

Kristen Woronoff

BLACKBIRCH PRESS

Detroit • New York • San Diego • San Francisco
Boston • New Haven, Conn. • Waterville, Maine
London • Munich

Published by Blackbirch Press
10911 Technology Place
San Diego, CA 92127
e-mail: customerservice@galegroup.com
Web site: http://www.galegroup.com/blackbirch

© 2002 Blackbirch Press
an imprint of the Gale Group

Printed in China

10 9 8 7 6 5 4 3 2 1

Photo credits:
Cover inset © Property of Blackbirch Press; cover, pages 3, 14, 17, 20, 22-23, 26-27, 28, 30 © CORBIS; pages 4-5 © The Library of Congress; pages 6, 8, 44 © AP/Wide World Photos; page 6 © Gerry Ellis/The Wildlife Collection; page 10 © P. Breese/Gamma-Liaison; page 10 © Ray Ellis/Photo Researchers, Inc.; page 13 © Bildarchiv Okapia/Photo Researchers, Inc.; page 16 © Tom McHugh/Photo Researchers, Inc.; page 19 © Hugo Van Lawick; page 29 © courtesy of Jane Goodall Institute

Library of Congress Cataloging-in-Publication Data
Woronoff, Kristen.
Jane Goodall / by Kristen Woronoff.
        p. cm. — (Famous women juniors)
Summary: A simple biography of the woman best known for her years studying chimpanzees in Africa.
        ISBN 1-56711-585-3 (hardcover : alk. paper)
1. Goodall, Jane, 1934 — Juvenile literature. 2. Primatologists—England—Biography—Juvenile literature. 3. Chimpanzees—Tanzania—Gombe Stream National Park—Juvenile literature. [1. Goodall, Jane, 1934- 2. Zoologists. 3. Women—Biography.] I. Title. II. Series.
QL31.G58 W67 2C02
590'.92—dc21
                                                              2001005126

Jane Goodall lived in Africa for more than 30 years. While she was there, she spent all her time studying chimpanzees. Her work led to important discoveries about chimpanzees.

3

Growing Up with Animals

Jane Goodall was born in London, England, on April 3, 1934. From the time she was a young child, she loved living creatures.

Jane's mother noticed how much her young daughter loved animals. Mrs. Goodall gave Jane a stuffed chimpanzee named Jubilee. It soon became Jane's favorite toy. She took it everywhere she went.

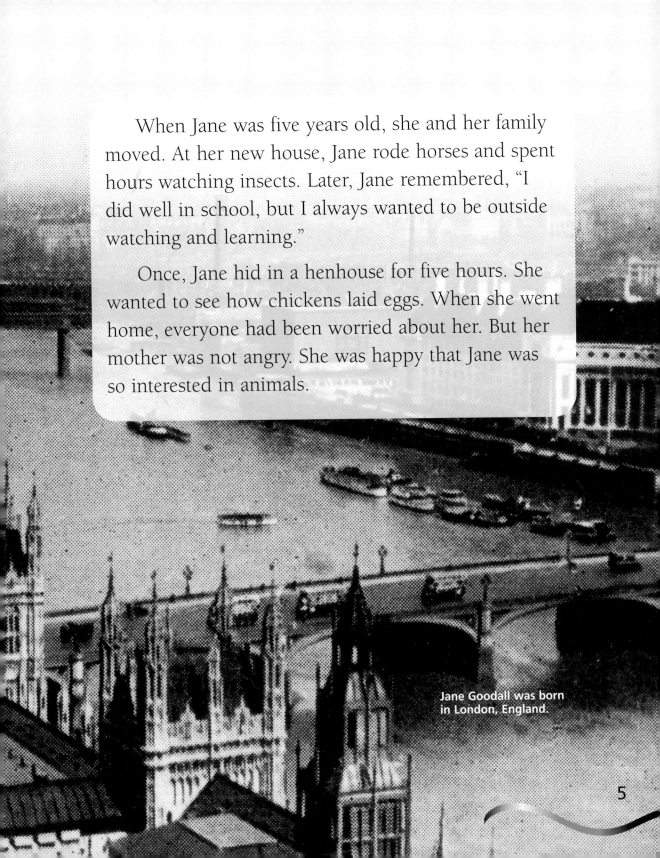

When Jane was five years old, she and her family moved. At her new house, Jane rode horses and spent hours watching insects. Later, Jane remembered, "I did well in school, but I always wanted to be outside watching and learning."

Once, Jane hid in a henhouse for five hours. She wanted to see how chickens laid eggs. When she went home, everyone had been worried about her. But her mother was not angry. She was happy that Jane was so interested in animals.

Jane Goodall was born in London, England.

5

Jane knew as a young girl that she someday wanted to go to Africa.

When Jane was seven years old, she read a book called *The Story of Dr. Dolittle*. Dr. Dolittle was an imaginary Englishman who lived in Africa. He could talk to animals. "I think that's when I first decided that someday I had to go to Africa," Jane later said.

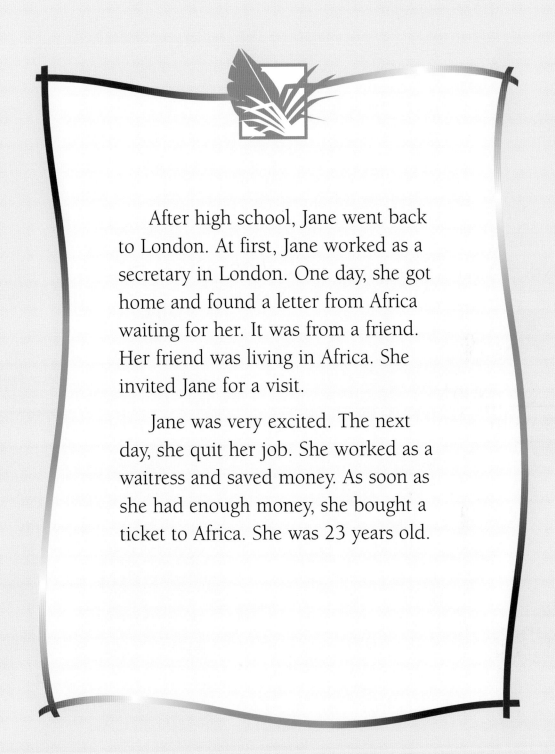

After high school, Jane went back to London. At first, Jane worked as a secretary in London. One day, she got home and found a letter from Africa waiting for her. It was from a friend. Her friend was living in Africa. She invited Jane for a visit.

Jane was very excited. The next day, she quit her job. She worked as a waitress and saved money. As soon as she had enough money, she bought a ticket to Africa. She was 23 years old.

A New Life

Jane flew to Kenya, a country in Africa, and stayed with a friend for several weeks. She was able to get a job as a secretary in Nairobi, the capital city of Kenya.

Jane had told her friend how much she liked animals. "If you like animals so much," her friend said, "then you should meet Dr. Leakey. He studies the bones of dead animals."

Dr. Louis Leakey was Jane's most important teacher.

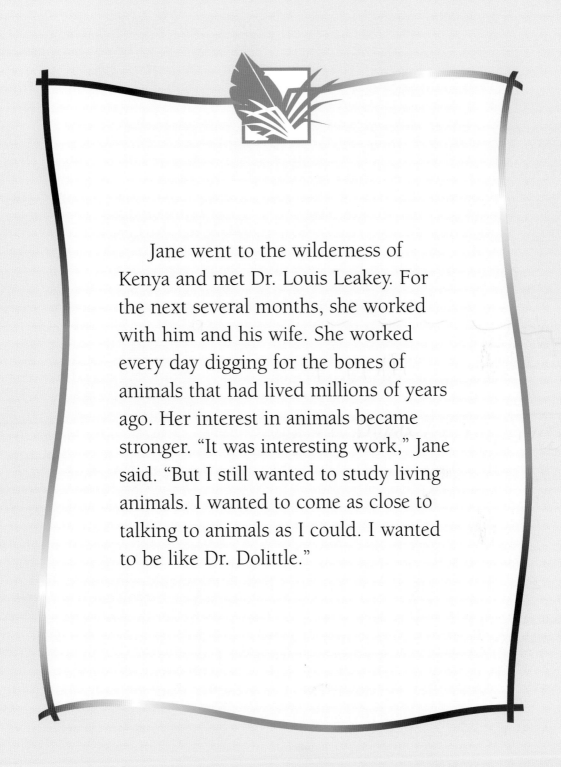

Jane went to the wilderness of Kenya and met Dr. Louis Leakey. For the next several months, she worked with him and his wife. She worked every day digging for the bones of animals that had lived millions of years ago. Her interest in animals became stronger. "It was interesting work," Jane said. "But I still wanted to study living animals. I wanted to come as close to talking to animals as I could. I wanted to be like Dr. Dolittle."

Jane got a job studying chimpanzees at the Gombe Stream Game Reserve.

Jane's interest in animals became obvious to Dr. Leakey as time went on. One day, he told Jane about a group of chimpanzees that had never been studied by humans before. He asked Jane if she wanted the job of studying them. She could hardly believe what she was hearing. This was exactly the kind of job Jane had always dreamed of!

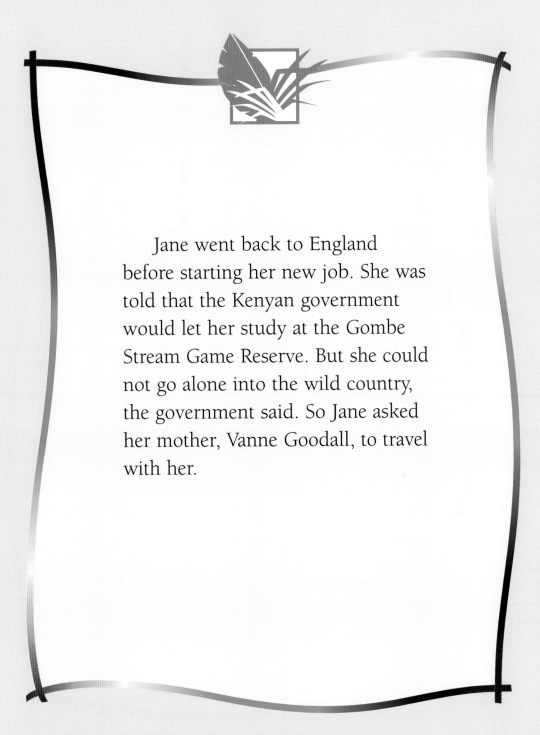

Jane went back to England
before starting her new job. She was
told that the Kenyan government
would let her study at the Gombe
Stream Game Reserve. But she could
not go alone into the wild country,
the government said. So Jane asked
her mother, Vanne Goodall, to travel
with her.

The two women arrived at the reserve in 1960. They had to take a two-hour boat ride on a river to get to their camp. As the boat chugged along, Jane watched the shore. She saw steep mountains rising from the water. In between the slopes were dense forests. Jane knew that she would have to explore those forests to find chimpanzees.

When Jane and her mother settled in at the camp, they met some of the native people who lived nearby. It was extremely hot in Africa. Jane and her mother did not have a refrigerator. They ate mostly baked beans, corned beef, and other canned foods. They slept on cots in tents.

As soon as they set up camp the first day they arrived, Jane slipped away alone. She wanted to explore the area around the camp. She climbed one of the high ridges. At the top, she could see for miles. That night, Jane put her cot outside of her tent. She wanted to sleep under the stars.

The next day, two local guides led Jane through the forest. They showed Jane places where chimpanzees ate fruit. The guides said the chimpanzees returned to the same spots every day.

Jane had to explore forests to find chimpanzees.

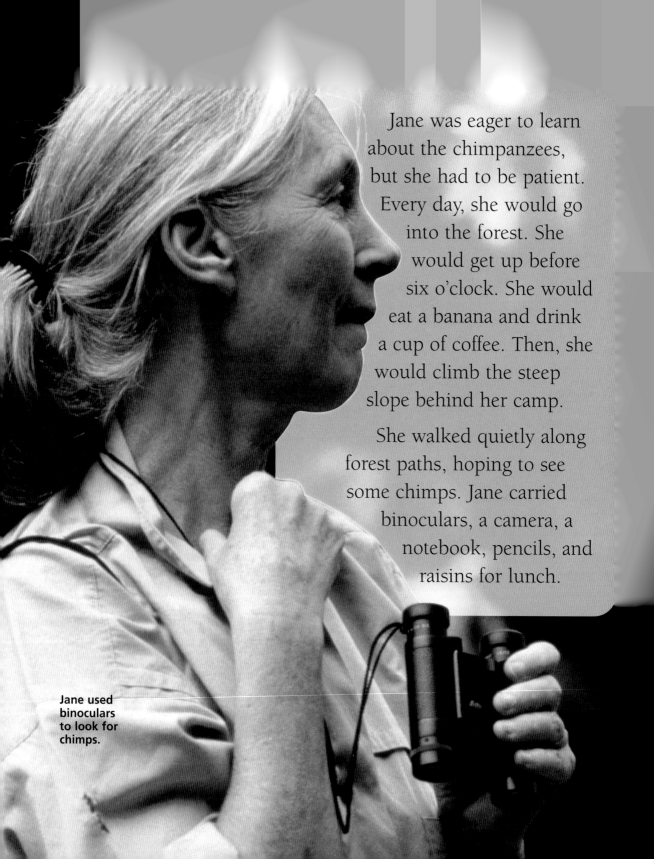

Jane was eager to learn about the chimpanzees, but she had to be patient. Every day, she would go into the forest. She would get up before six o'clock. She would eat a banana and drink a cup of coffee. Then, she would climb the steep slope behind her camp.

She walked quietly along forest paths, hoping to see some chimps. Jane carried binoculars, a camera, a notebook, pencils, and raisins for lunch.

Jane used binoculars to look for chimps.

She waited for the chimps for weeks and months, but she rarely saw them. Jane was discouraged. She was afraid she would never get close enough to these animals to learn about them. But she was learning about the forest in other ways. Her skin became hardened against the rough grasses. She knew her way around the forest, and she learned how to recognize different animal tracks.

Jane would not return to camp until late at night. And when she returned, she would continue to work. She would eat dinner and copy her notes. Sometimes she would not get to sleep until after midnight.

After many months, Jane finally saw some chimps.

Meeting the Chimps

For many months, Jane had trouble getting close to any chimpanzees. One morning, she looked up at the mountain behind her camp. She decided to climb it and see if there were any chimps living at the top.

When she got to the top, she saw three chimps staring at her! They did not run away. They didn't even move for several minutes. Then, they slowly walked into the bushes. Later, more chimps came near Jane. They were eating figs. They saw Jane, let out a few loud calls, and then continued to eat.

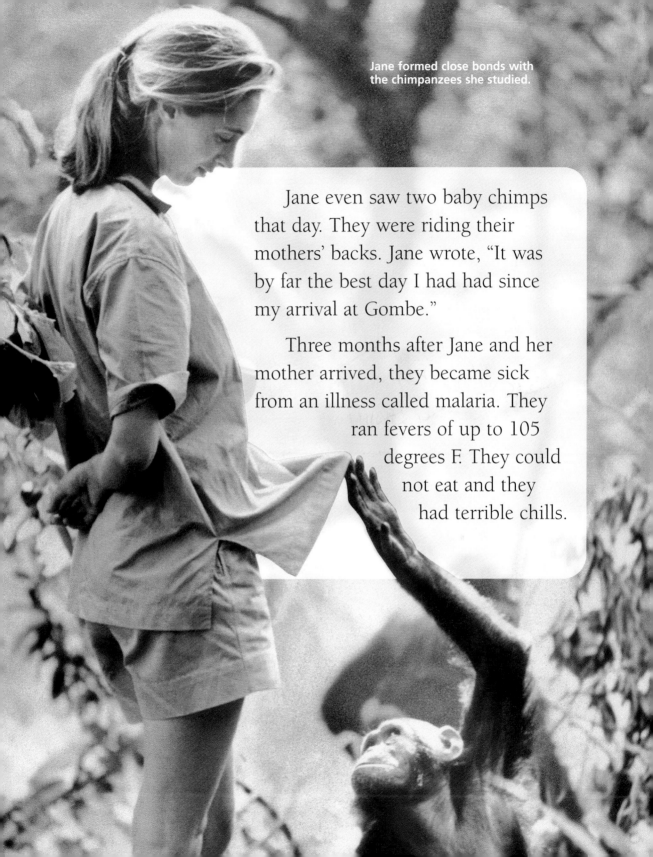

Jane formed close bonds with the chimpanzees she studied.

Jane even saw two baby chimps that day. They were riding their mothers' backs. Jane wrote, "It was by far the best day I had had since my arrival at Gombe."

Three months after Jane and her mother arrived, they became sick from an illness called malaria. They ran fevers of up to 105 degrees F. They could not eat and they had terrible chills.

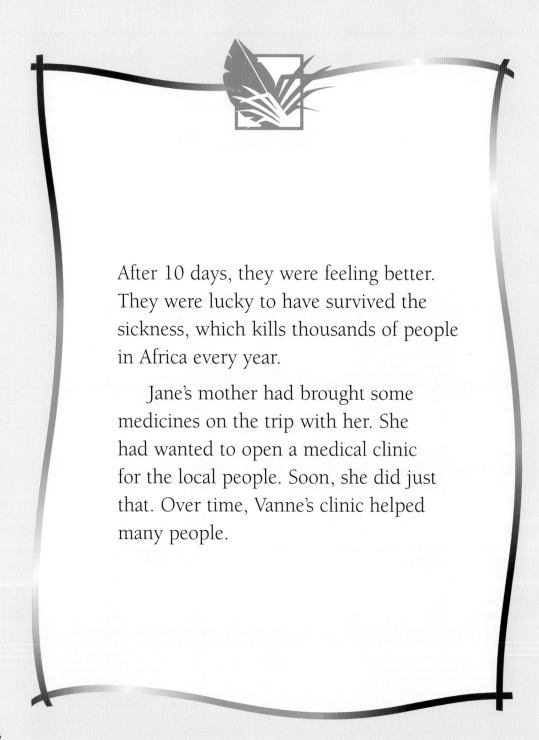

After 10 days, they were feeling better. They were lucky to have survived the sickness, which kills thousands of people in Africa every year.

Jane's mother had brought some medicines on the trip with her. She had wanted to open a medical clinic for the local people. Soon, she did just that. Over time, Vanne's clinic helped many people.

Jane gave names to the chimps she studied.

As the days passed, the chimps got used to Jane being around them. She even camped near them so she could watch them early in the morning.

Jane realized that chimps were different from each other. Like humans, they had special habits and personalities. She decided to give them names. Some of the names were Mrs. Maggs, Spray, Mr. Worzle, Mr. McGregor, and Count Dracula.

Jane was surprised to find the chimps were not afraid of her at all.

For two months, Jane watched the chimps from the top of the mountain. Then she started to move closer to get a better look at them. Jane was surprised that the chimps were not afraid of her at all. Instead, they were curious about her. But their curiosity was dangerous. Instead of running away from her, they would stare at her. One time, a group surrounded her. They shook the branches around Jane and showed signs of anger. Then, they simply walked away.

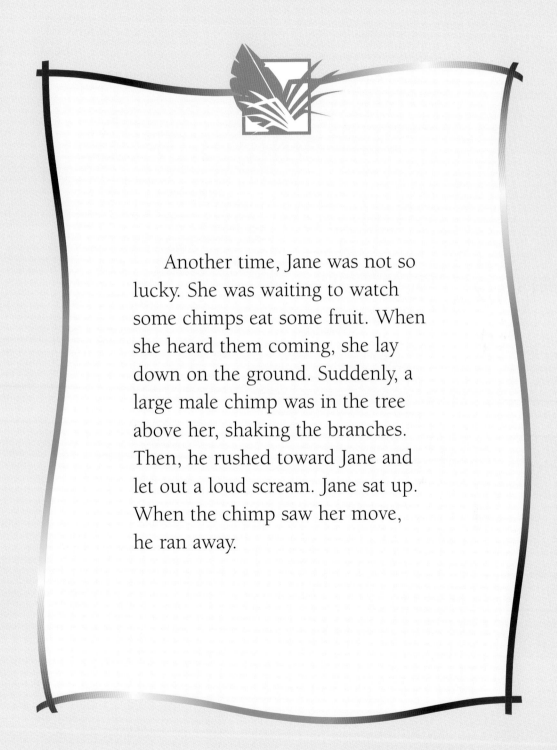

Another time, Jane was not so lucky. She was waiting to watch some chimps eat some fruit. When she heard them coming, she lay down on the ground. Suddenly, a large male chimp was in the tree above her, shaking the branches. Then, he rushed toward Jane and let out a loud scream. Jane sat up. When the chimp saw her move, he ran away.

Soon Jane began to feel strong bonds with the chimps. One day, she was sitting near a chimp she called David Graybeard. She saw a nut on the ground. Jane picked it up and held it out for the chimp. He looked at the fruit. Then he reached out and held Jane's hand. That was the beginning of a caring friendship between Jane and David.

Through her work, Jane made important discoveries about how chimps eat. She discovered that chimpanzees do not only eat fruits and vegetables. She found that they sometimes eat other animals. She also learned that chimps make and use tools. They use curled-up leaves as drinking cups, for example. No one knew this before Jane wrote about it.

Later Life

In 1962, a man named Hugo Van Lawick arrived at the camp. He had been sent to take pictures of Jane and the chimps. Jane and Hugo discovered they had much in common and soon fell in love. They were married in London in 1964.

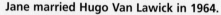

Jane married Hugo Van Lawick in 1964.

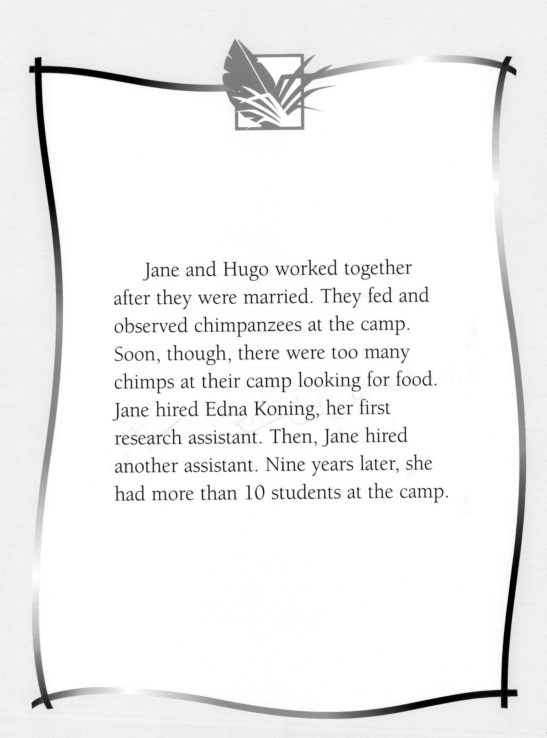

Jane and Hugo worked together after they were married. They fed and observed chimpanzees at the camp. Soon, though, there were too many chimps at their camp looking for food. Jane hired Edna Koning, her first research assistant. Then, Jane hired another assistant. Nine years later, she had more than 10 students at the camp.

In 1966, Jane and Hugo became the parents of a baby boy. They nicknamed him "Grub." As Grub grew older, Jane and Hugo did not think he was safe at the camp. They were afraid the chimps might bother him. For a while, they kept Grub in a cage for safety. When the boy was nine years old, he was sent to a boarding school in England. For Jane it was a sad time. Not only had her son gone away, David Graybeard, one of Jane's

Jane and her research assistants pose for a photographer.

favorite chimpanzees, had stopped coming around. Jane knew he had died.

In 1974, Jane and Hugo were divorced. Jane later married a man named Derek Bryceson.

As more assistants came to the reserve, Jane allowed them to work alone. But first she taught them how to follow the chimps and what information to record.

Jane decided to do more to help save the world's chimps.

Soon sadness struck again. Jane's husband, Derek, died of cancer. She felt alone and discouraged. But after spending time with her family in England, Jane returned to Gombe.

When she returned, Jane spent many hours in the forests. As much as she loved the work, Jane knew that she had to do more. Chimps in other parts of Africa were being killed or were dying out. She had watched only the Gombe chimps for so long. Now it was time to think about chimps in other lands.

In 1977, Jane founded the Jane Goodall Institute in Tucson, Arizona. The purpose of the institute is to help save the world's chimpanzees. Jane now lectures once a month at the institute. She also raises money to help buy land that can be set aside to protect chimpanzees.

Jane founded the Jane Goodall Institute in Tucson, Arizona in 1977.

The Jane Goodall Institute

Jane's work has led to a greater understanding of chimps and their behavior.

"Chimps are thinking, feeling beings," Jane often says in her lectures. She also visits chimps that are kept in laboratories for research. She makes sure they are not mistreated. Scientists use chimps because they are more like humans than any other living creatures. Jane has sadly accepted the need for chimps in medical research. But she is always speaking out about the need for better conditions for them. Fortunately, some researchers are taking her advice.

Jane Goodall has spent most her life in the wild areas of Kenya. She has learned more about chimpanzees than anyone knew before. She hopes that her work will help keep us understand these special creatures. If we understand them, we can help to keep these animals safe and protected for a long time to come.

Glossary

Dense Thick.

Malaria A severe disease that is spread by the bite of mosquitoes.

Native Belonging to a place by birth.

Reserve Land set aside for endangered animals.

Wilderness Undeveloped land.

For More Information

Websites

The Jane Goodall Institute
www.janegoodall.org

This comprehensive, official website includes the biography of Goodall, information on chimpanzees and the Institute, and tips on how to join in creating a safe space for chimpanzees.

Books

Goodall, Jane. *The Chimpanzee Family Book.* Coral Gables, FL: North-South Books, 1997.

January, Brendan. *Jane Goodall: Animal Behaviorist and Writer.* Chicago: Ferguson Publishing, 2001.

Meechum, Virginia. *Jane Goodall: Protector of Chimpanzees.* Berkeley Heights, NJ: Enslow Publishers, 1997.

Pettit, Jayne. *Jane Goodall: Pioneer Researcher.* Dabury, CT: Franklin Watts, 1999.

Index

DATE DUE

	JUN 2 5 2013		

Stamford Community Library
986 Main Road
Stamford, VT 05352
802-694-1379